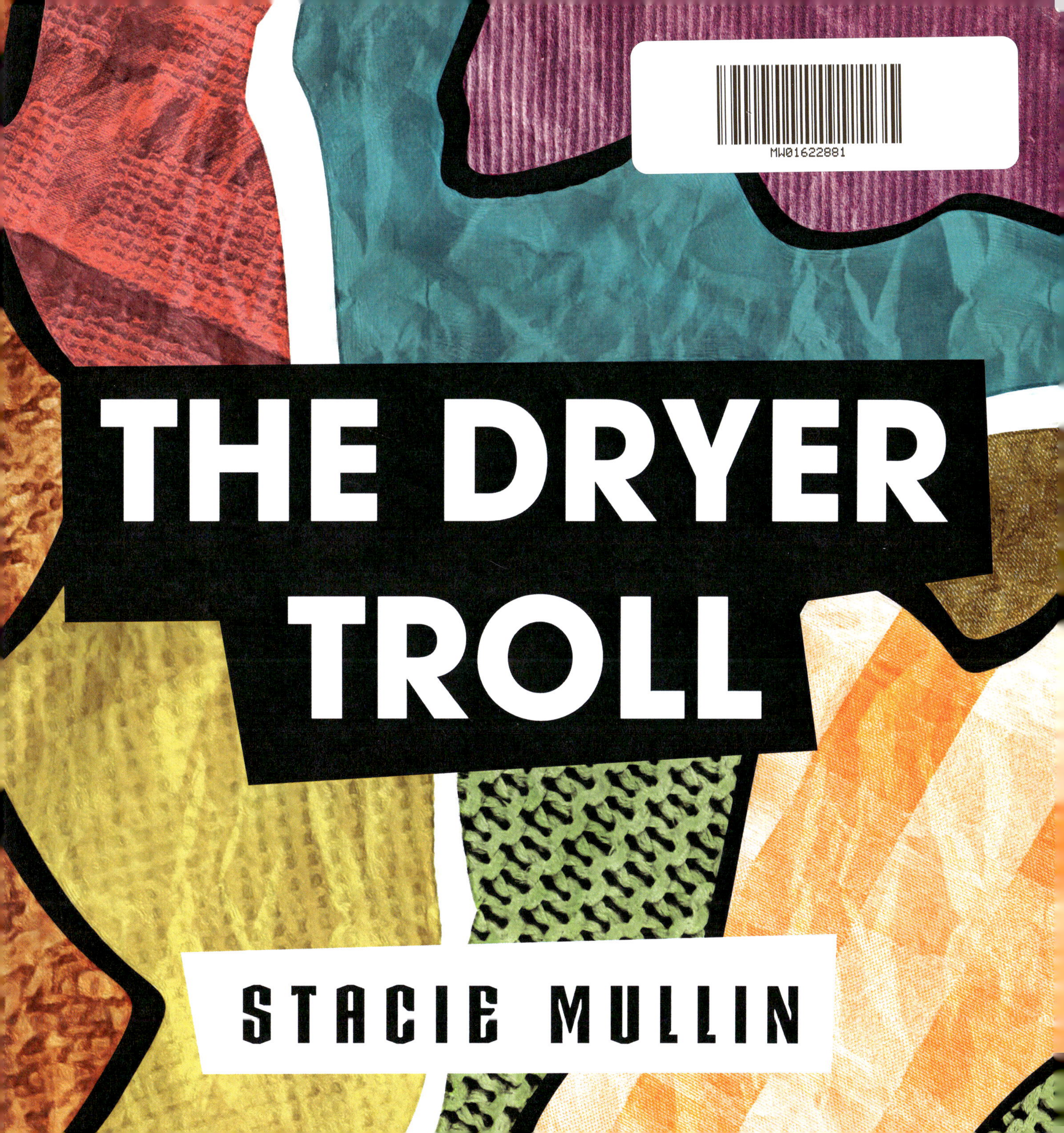
MW01622881
THE DRYER
TROLL
STACIE MULLIN

Torn Curtain Publishing
Wellington, New Zealand
www.torncurtainpublishing.com

ISBN Softcover: 978-0-6451757-6-9
ISBN Hardcover: 978-0-6451757-7-6

Typeset in ITC Avant Garde Gothic Pro, Taurunum Ferrum

Illustrations by Ella Paramore. Used with permission.

Cataloging in Publishing Data
Title: The Dryer Troll
Subjects: Juvenile fiction, Imagination and play, Monsters, Trolls, Fantasy
Author: Stacie Mullin

A copy of this book is held at the National Library of the United States of America.

I dedicate this book to my daughters Emily and Nicole, and also to my husband Jeremy. Without you all there would be no Dryer Troll.

Way deep down in a dark damp place,

lives a very gross troll

with a monstrous face.

He is covered in hair from head to toe,

And if only you could see him
it would make for quite a show.

You may not ever catch him
—but we all know he is there,

And the reason

that we know this

is . . .

our socks

have lost

their pairs!

In case you think it's silly,
let me try to explain

because I'm sure you think it sounds a little bit insane!

I put a pair of socks
in the dryer
where it's hot

But only one comes out.

That is weird,

is it not?

I am sure a troll is hiding somewhere in my dryer vent,

crouched beneath a hairball,
or in his own lint tent.

I bet that ugly troll has made a house
out of my socks,

and if only I could find him,
I would walk right up and knock.

There'd be socks of all the colors,

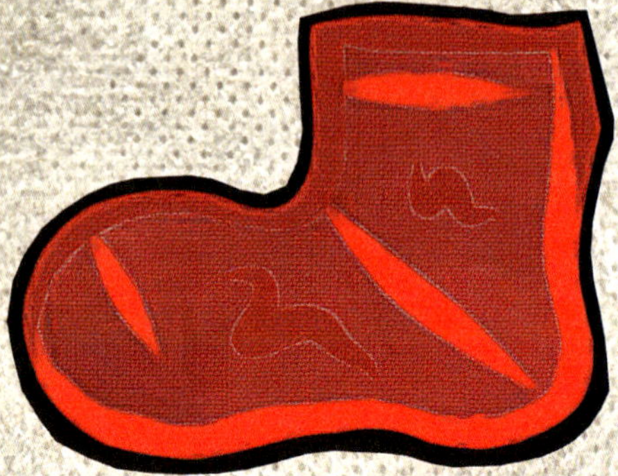

blue and yellow,
white, and red.

And I'd find them mixed together

in an orange sock bed!

That troll may have a
son,
or a daughter
and a wife,

And I have no doubt at all that they're living the good life.

I search for that troll
in the dryer
every day,

And
I think of him
in my bed
while
I
lay.

Sometimes I try to sneak in at night,

Hoping to catch him,
I flick on
the light.

But I have not caught a glimpse of him
to show you in this book,

So for now we can only guess
how he must look.

He may be short and plump,
or skinny, or hairy.

And I imagine he may be

So when
you look in
in
the
dryer
to find a
missing sock,

Just be ready! If you see him,

he may give you
quite a SHOCK!

ABOUT THE AUTHOR

I was born and raised in Florida and currently live on the East Coast. I am married and have two daughters. I have been writing children's stories since I was ten years old. The Dryer Troll is my very first published story. Currently, I am battling stage 4 breast cancer, and have been for a year. I'm so thankful that my story can finally be enjoyed by children everywhere. It's such a wonderful legacy to leave for my children. God bless you all.

- Stacie Mullin

Made in United States
North Haven, CT
07 January 2023